50 THINGS
YOUR REAL ESTATE AGENT
SHOULD TELL YOU,
BUT PROBABLY WON'T!

To my
Real Estate
Sister!
Keep Teaching
+
Leading!

50 THINGS
YOUR REAL ESTATE AGENT
SHOULD TELL YOU,
BUT PROBABLY WON'T!

Tips from an experienced real estate agent that will shorten your learning curve in the world of buying, selling, investing, or managing real estate

ALLEN JOHNSON

Icons made by Freepik from www.flaticon.com

CONTENTS

Introduction   1

BUYER BEWARE

#1 Steps to Buying a Home That 99 Percent of Home Buyers
Don't Even Focus On   5

#2 Art of Negotiating   7

#3 Secrets *Realtors* Use When They Buy Their Own Homes   9

#4 Selling or Buying Under Pressure Could Cost You   11

#5 Repairs vs. Renovations   13

#6 Secrets Most New Home Builders *Don't* Want You to Know   15

#7 New Home Doesn't Equal Perfect Home   17

HOW TO BE A SMART SELLER

#8 Tips for a First-Time Seller   21

#9 The True Process of Selling a Home   23

#10 The Risk of Overpricing Your Home   25

#11 Commission Doesn't Matter   27

#12 Sellers: Get Comfortable Being Uncomfortable   28

#13 The First Offer Is the Best Offer   30

#14 When the Highest Offer Isn't the Best Offer   32

HOW TO BE A SMART SELLER (CONTINUED)

#15 The Silliest Things Can Kill a Real Estate Deal   34

#16 The One Percent Rule to Negotiating Home Inspections Properly   36

#17 Secrets Agents Use When They Sell Their Own Homes   38

MASTERY OF THE BASICS OF REAL ESTATE

#18 Finding Your Perfect Piece of Real Estate   43

#19 You Can't Time the Market   45

#20 Choosing Relationships Over Short-Term Gains   47

#21 Get Credit Before You Need Credit   49

#22 The "C" Word: Commissions, Commissions, Commissions   51

#23 The Young Person's Plan for Real Estate Wealth   54

#24 Three Vital Lessons You Should Teach Your Kids About Real Estate   56

#25 In the End, It Will All Make Sense   58

HIRING THE RIGHT PROFESSIONAL

#26 How Do You *Know* When You Have a Great Agent   63

#27 A Great Agent Is Your Best Friend   65

#28 You Hire Me to Help You Make Decisions   67

#29 There Are No Real Estate Schools for Real Estate Agents   69

#30 What We Get Paid Doesn't Matter   72

#31 Jack of All Trades and Master of None   74

#32 You're Being Unreasonable   76

#33 Real Estate Ain't Sexy   78

#34 I Can't Save You   80

#35 Why Your Agent Lies to You   82

TACKLING RENOVATIONS & REPAIRS

#36 Quality Matters   89

#37 Mrs. and Mr. Do-It-Yourself-er   91

#38 Renovating to Sell vs. Renovating to Rent   93

#39 How to Pick a Good, Reliable Contractor   95

PROTECTING YOUR INVESTMENT/LANDLORD 101

#40 The Perfect Rental Property   99

#41 Should I Rent or Sell My Home?   101

#42 Tips for Turning Over Your Rental Property   103

#43 Preventive Maintenance on a Rental Property   105

#44 It's All Good Until It's Not   107

#45 Give Grace   109

#46 The Devil Is in the Details   111

#47 Build Your Team Before You Need Your *Need* Your Team   113

#48 Flipping vs. Buying and Holding   115

#49 The Four Ways to Make Money in Real Estate Investing   118

PAY IT FORWARD

#50 Why Real Estate—My Story   123

Be a Blessing Foundation   127

INTRODUCTION

I've had the honor and privilege of selling more than 1,000 homes and investing in over $20 million in real estate. I was a top producing agent during both the height of the real estate market and during the historic crash. I've represented multimillionaires and young couples saving for their first home. The Northern Virginia area is one the most diverse in the country, and it's been a blessing to work with clients and friends from all over the world. This experience has given me a wealth of knowledge and understanding about real estate holistically. I've always been more concerned with teaching and learning real estate than selling it. I figured if I knew more about it, then selling it would come more easily. It's worked well for me, and now I'm on a mission to educate those that are interested in understanding this wonderful world of real estate. Now, I must warn you, I'm an acquired taste. I'm not for everyone. Some want their proverbial coffee with sugar and cream, and I'm more like a straight cup of coffee, strong and black. But if you like it straight up with no chaser, then I'm your guy. I've decided to donate all the proceeds from the success of this book to our foundation.

If you'd like to learn more about what this blessing of a life in real estate has allowed us to do, check out our website at www.AllenJohnsonCoaching.com.

Welcome to my thoughts, advice, opinions, muses, and critique of real estate—real life.

BUYER BEWARE

STEPS TO BUYING A HOME THAT 99 PERCENT OF HOME BUYERS DON'T EVEN FOCUS ON

Mindset is first! You have to have a desire to buy a home. It's not easy in today's market, so you have to have a big *WHY*. Are you buying for wealth, long-term retirement planning, monthly income, finally moving out of the basement, or for your growing family and kids? Your *why* will always drive your *how*.

Game planning is the next step. Buying a home is more competitive and complicated than ever. Asking and answering the difficult questions up front will eliminate discomfort in the process. The best questions your agent can ask you are usually insightful ones about how you operate, such as, "How do you typically make big decisions?" and "What will likely keep you up at night regarding this process?" Some things you can do to help yourself out during this process are as follows:

- **Find an agent with whom you can be completely honest.** You will need someone that will stick with you in the ups and downs of the process. Spending this much money is inherently stressful. Most people don't handle the stress well. I give my clients permission to vent to me.

- **Understand your numbers.** What you can afford versus what you want to afford are often two different numbers. It's too late to understand the difference in the midst of negotiations. Negotiations are the most emotional time of the home buying process. Your numbers should already be locked in. This will keep you from making a financial decision that you will regret later.

- **Get to know the neighborhoods before you find the house.** That can be done without your agent. Drive around on weekends and get a vibe of the neighborhood. Ask yourself, "Can you imagine yourself living in this neighborhood?" Agents can't legally answer the question, "Is this a good neighborhood?" Besides, one person's definition of good maybe very different than yours.

- **Narrow your focus.** You should be able to do a majority of that online. With pictures and virtual tours, you can save time and eliminate the homes that don't fit your criteria. If it doesn't look good in pictures, it likely won't look good in person. The average home buyer is physically walking into six homes or fewer before they are writing an offer.

- **Be prepared to make an offer.** Review the contract and procedures before you write an offer. When the perfect home hits the market, you have very little time to ask questions. Schedule an up-front buyer's consultation to go over the basics. When you're thinking about offer price, terms, and inspections, there's often a timeline to get the offer into the seller's hands. Do as much work as you can up front.

- **Lastly, enjoy the process!** It's stressful, but you don't buy a home every day. When things get challenging, remember your big *why*. Imagine the memories and good times you will have in that perfect home.

THE ART OF NEGOTIATING

When negotiating a real estate deal, *leverage* is everything. Leverage is created in many different ways. It's in the questions you ask. It's in the questions you answer. It's in positioning your offer to sell or buy. It's in the timing you decide to sell or buy. The leverage is in the details.

Examples:

- If a BUYER visits your home more than once before the deal is finalized, they have essentially told you that they really, really, really like the property.

- If you visit a new home sales representative and tell them that it's your first time buying a home, this could be a good leverage strategy if you have done it before. But if this is your first time, watch how you answer questions. Your answers should be truthful but never show all your cards, think about turning their questions into conversations. Conversations lead to opportunities.

- If you go to an open house and you tell the seller's agent that your lease is up at the end of the month and you can't stand your landlord, the timing is now on the seller's side because they know your urgency.

- Your agent tipping personal and seemingly unimportant details that alert the other agent to desire, financial means, and desperation could put leverage in favor of the other agent.

AJ REAL-LIFE EXAMPLE:
I had a home that was on the market for longer than I'd like. I get a call from an agent that has an interested buyer. They are from out of state. The agent does a video conference for the buyer and tells me that they are planning to fly in to see the home. If a client is booking a flight in to see a home, the odds are that they are committed to getting a deal done. That info netted our sellers an extra $5K that we never would've countered without that small, seemingly unimportant detail.

The bottom line is getting the best real estate deal is often found in the details. Make sure your realtor coaches you *before* you visit properties. One question answered incorrectly can kill your leverage. Negotiating a real estate deal is more of an art than a science.

AJ Bonus Tip:
Never speak about a home you are visiting while inside the property. With advancements in technology like Ring and Alexa, you never know who is listening or watching.

SECRETS *REALTORS* USE WHEN THEY BUY THEIR OWN HOMES

Would you follow the lead of someone that didn't know where they were going? No.

What about advice from someone that never went through the situation that you're about to go through? Likely *not*.

Would you take advice from a professional who's at the top of their game, who went through the exact situation that you find yourself? MOST DEFINITELY.

There are many tricks and tips out there. We have focused on a few secrets that successful, top-producing agents use when they buy and sell their personal homes.

These are a few of my personal buyer secrets:

- **Put a timeline deadline on offers**, normally 36 to 48 hours. Now this only works if you plan to write a FAIR offer. This technique can be risky, but it can also force the seller to make a decision, instead of waiting to see what other offers might come in. Every seller fears a loss, and this timeline puts the fear of loss right in front of the homeowner. What if I don't get a higher offer? Should I wait? Will this buyer wait? We are really looking to get the seller and their agent thinking, engaging, responding, and prayerfully accepting our offer.

- **Always have flexibility with financing.** Successful agents have access to different types of loan programs, so they can switch their financing if the right deal calls for it. I shop lenders for loan programs, rather than focusing solely on rates. I know that the right loan program can make all the difference when buying a home. Imagine two offers on the same home. Both are the same price, terms, same everything, but one offer is putting down a little bit more (e.g., 3.5% vs. 5%). The seller is likely to accept the offer with more money down, all other things being equal. Digging in on the available loan programs and possible sources of extra down payment has won me several great properties.

- **View homes during the week and write offers fast.** The key is making sure the potential seller sees the offer before the weekend starts. Successful agents want to get a good offer in the seller's hand before the weekend competition. If it's a good home, by the time it hits the weekend, it's too late. Activity will likely drive the price up. Be early!

- **Speaking of early, always start early**. I never want to be controlled by a timeline. I know that the perfect home is never on my timeline. That perfect home is always on the seller's timeline and when they decide to list and sell their home. I start looking and writing offers months before I need to move or invest.

SELLING OR BUYING UNDER PRESSURE COULD COST YOU

Most people wait until they have to move to make a decision. They buy when their lease is over, sell when they decide to retire, or move when the school year ends. Now, some of these time constraints are unavoidable. But others are flexible and, if flexed properly, can end up making your real estate buying or selling process more profitable.

We had a young couple that wanted to buy their first home. They were renting a townhome, and the lease didn't end until June. Starting their home search 10 months early and getting educated on the process was important to them as it was their first time and they were spending the most money they've ever spent! One of their biggest concerns was having to pay for the lease and mortgage at the same time. During our meeting, we discovered that the landlord for their current place would be open to letting them out of their lease if he or they could find someone to replace their term of the lease. It worked out well for our clients because shopping in the winter means less competition and more opportunity to get a better deal and more closing costs (which most first-time buyers sorely need). In this case, their flexibility worked to their advantage.

I've also seen countless cases of sellers nearing retirement waiting until the last minute to buy their future retirement home. In most cases, those that start the downsizing early and create a solid plan, end up in a more profitable position.

Since most retirees income will naturally decrease after they stop working, every dollar saved is a dollar earned.

If moving is somewhere in your upcoming life horizon, make sure to prepare early. Try to find time contingencies and flexibility. Those that can find that margin set themselves up for more profit, and in real estate, more money is good.

REPAIRS VS. RENOVATIONS

Imagine the following: You saved money for your down payment, went through the painfully long process of getting the bank all of your documents for your preapproval, spent months on various websites searching for the perfect home, wrote offers only to lose a few, got off from work during the middle of the day to see a home that just came on the market, worried about finally getting the home of your dreams, and you finally got it! (There's a bunch of things that happen between this point and getting your keys, but I'll save that for another day.)

Now you have the keys to your dream home; you're happy, your family's happy, and you move into your dream home! Everything is going great, but you see a small leak coming from the ceiling. You clean it up and think nothing else about it. You're busy, working to pay off this home. A month later, you see the same leak and clean it again. You finally get your handyman (brother-in-law) to come look at the problem, and now you have a full-scale roof or plumbing project on your hands. This wasn't in the video, or the paperwork, or ever discussed by your agent. But this is the reality of owning a home. Repairs are much more important to the long-term value of your home than renovations. Repairs often aren't found until they became bigger than they need to do be. The basics of your home should be inspected visually by you once per month. Some areas to inspect:

- **Plumbing:** Look up at the ceiling, under and around toilets and bathroom vanities, under and around kitchen sinks; look at and test your sump pump. When you know a sump pump has failed, it's too late, and you likely have water somewhere you don't want it.

- **Electrical:** Open your panel. Test a few outlets.

- **Structural:** Take a walk around your house. Do you see anything like water settling? Make sure all downspouts are connected, and gutters are clean. This is the number one reason water gets into basements. Any cracks in the foundation? We've seen cracks in homes that are only three years old!

- **Roof:** Make sure no shingles are missing. Take a peek in the attic and see if there are any watermarks.

- **HVAC:** Get it serviced twice a year by a qualified technician, even if it's running fine.

This is a small checklist of things, but it doesn't represent everything required to take care of your investment. Notice I didn't say home. It's actually an asset, and it needs to be taken care of properly to appreciate in value.

So many buyers focus on renovations, but not so much on repairs. It's your responsibility as a seller and owner to find repairs before they become costly and major.

I know your agent didn't want to be a buzzkill at the settlement table, but I'm here to tell you: Owning a home is work. Don't let me start on preventive maintenance on a rental property.

SECRETS MOST NEW HOME BUILDERS *DON'T* WANT YOU TO KNOW

(FIVE THINGS YOU *MUST* KNOW BEFORE YOU VISIT A *NEW* CONSTRUCTION SALES OFFICE)

Over the past 17 years, I've been blessed to sell more than 1,000 homes in many different markets. Our team has worked with many builders in many different price points and product categories. These are the tips that have given our clients an advantage when buying new construction:

- **They pay for you to work with a real estate professional.** In fact, they welcome and encourage you to work with a *good* real estate professional. There are so many decisions that need to be made during the process, having someone that's "been there and done that" can take away a lot of unnecessary anxiety. When you add stress to large amounts of money, anything can happen.

- **You will get a better deal with a high-volume, local real estate agent.** YOU represent one deal and one home. A high-volume, local agent will likely bring multiple buyers, thus multiple homes. The increased volume means the likelihood of better deals for their clients and more opportunities for the builder.

- **Most homes are now built in a factory, not on-site anymore.** Thus, customizations from volume builders are very rare and extremely costly. Make sure you know what you want before you sign the contract.

- **The sales representative represents the builder.** The sales representative is paid by the builder, so they are super experienced, but not about what matters for you! Most don't know much about the overall real estate market. Many have never seen other comparable homes outside of their new home site. They may know their product well, but rarely understand the bigger picture and how your new home fits into that picture. Ask them about real estate trends. Have they walked into other comparable properties? What's the best way to increase property value?

- **Home inspections and radon inspections are vital to anyone buying a new home.** I can show you inspection lists from recently built new homes that would make you cringe. Everything from mold, electrical, and plumbing to toxic levels of radon. New home builders won't encourage you to get these inspections. Not that they are trying to hide anything, but everyone makes mistakes. You need an extra set of eyes when you are spending this much money.

- **It's *all* about the LOT.** There will be many homes that are the same model in a new home community, but there will only be very few prime lots. The old adage rings true in all types of real estate: location, location, location. This is where a good real estate professional is worth their expertise. Not only comparing lots in the new build neighborhood, but also comparing other surrounding neighborhoods. I've recently seen same home on different lots differ by $20K or more in market value!

NEW HOME DOESN'T EQUAL PERFECT HOME

I've seen and negotiated thousands of home inspections. Some homes were new, some were fixer-uppers, and most were somewhere in between. The commonality found in all homes are that NONE are perfect.

A new home built specifically for our buyer had mold issues in the basement. Not due to the way it was built, but the way it was managed when it was built.

A 20-year-old single family home purchased by a single man that didn't have time for basic yearly maintenance had two pages of major issues: roof, structural, electrical, plumbing, and more.

A condo close to the city, normally with easy inspection items, had electrical panel issues and needed a hot water heater replacement.

I would say that 90 percent of any problems in a home are due to neglect and poor homeownership habits. Owning a home is work. It requires you to literally do work after you finish your nine-to-five job. If you think you can come home, relax, and do nothing, check nothing, or maintain nothing over an extended period of time, you will end up paying for it in the end. I've seen it happen too many times. As you have heard me say before, your home is an investment and should be treated as such.

Therefore, anyone buying a home should expect problems, maintenance issues, and things that need to be fixed. There is no home that is perfect. Understand that every home will have some repairs or issues that you will need to deal with when you're planning to buy it. Don't be surprised, do your homework, assess the issues, lean on your agent's expertise, and negotiate to have the owner fix the items or have them credit you to fix them after you move in.

Home inspections are often the most volatile and emotional time of any real estate transaction. Make sure you're level headed and realistic. Don't let your feelings and a little due diligence keep you from your perfect home.

AJ BONUS TIP:
Sellers, you can't fix everything when you are selling your home, but you can fix maintenance issues. If you don't know where to begin, hire a third-party to inspect your home. Start there, and it will save you a lot of surprises down the road.

HOW TO BE A SMART SELLER

TIPS FOR A FIRST-TIME SELLER

We often focus on first-time buyers. There are programs, TV shows, informational pamphlets, books, and YouTube and Vimeo videos that have tons of tips at your fingertips. But what about the person that is selling the most expensive asset they have likely ever owned? Don't worry; I got you and haven't forgotten how stressful this side of the process can be. Here are some tips to consider:

- **Start early!** The process of selling a home should start just as early, if not *earlier*, than buying your first home. When I say early, I mean at least a year before you need to move. Repairs that can only be done in good weather, cosmetic upgrades that you may need time to get quotes on, talking to your agent to make sure the things you're doing make sense and will make you money, coordinating contractors, and planning where you want to move next. There are so many moving parts; the most successful and stress-free sellers start early.

- **Don't take it personally.** Once you put your home on the market, this is a business transaction. All the memories and great things you have done to your home may not be important to the next buyer. Get out of your feelings, step back, and make smart decisions. Emotionally driven decisions often end up making less money and creating more stress in the end.

- **Understand the buyer profile.** If you are a first-time seller, then the most likely person buying your home now is a first-time buyer. Remember back to when you purchased that home. You were nervous, right? Did you have a lot of questions? Did you have a lot of cash on hand? Did small things, now in retrospect, look big? The same issues that you went through when you bought your home are the same issues the next buyer is likely facing. Plan accordingly; let this be your guide to questions you may have. The only difference between them and you is they are likely paying more than you did when you purchased.

- **Do what your agent tells you to do.** (Granted, they must be a good agent for this rule to apply!) Realize this is your first time selling a home, but your agent does this *every day*. Lean on them during this time. If you have a question, make sure to ask it. Don't let an easy question tumble into a sleepless night. If your agent tells you to repair something, do it. If your agent tells you to counter a low offer, do it. If your agent tells you to lower your price or not to lower your price, do it. You have hired a professional; trust in their wisdom and experience to guide you to the finish line. You may not understand it or agree with it during the process, but it will all make sense in the end.

THE TRUE PROCESS OF SELLING A HOME

The most important factor to you selling your home is not your agent! It's actually your home. Buyers don't buy agents, nor do they even care about your agent. They care the most about your home and if it will meet their needs, wants, desires, and expectations. Thus, the most important job is to get your home ready for the market. That process should start years before you decide to sell. Most sellers don't do the up-front work that makes the selling process easier.

Maintenance items are things that you should, at minimum, be handling on a quarterly basis. Is your heating and cooling serviced and maintained properly? Are the roof, gutters, windows, and outside trim looking good and updated? Are your bathrooms and kitchen caulked properly? Any leaks or electrical outlets loose or needing attention? There are many more questions that can be highlighted, but these are a good start.

The problem I see the most with sellers is they let these issues pile up, and it costs too much and takes too much time to get them corrected when it comes time to sell. They cannot even get to the next most important factor, which is cosmetic, because they never maintained the house properly.

This leads me to the above-mentioned cosmetic upgrades. Ninety percent of the time I find that our sellers' design tastes are not what buyers want. The paint might be nice, but the flooring isn't jiving. The kitchen looks nice, but the bathrooms could use some new tiles. It's up to your agent's market knowledge and expertise to tell you what's needed and what is not. You should not be making these types of decisions on your own. When I'm selling my own home (and I've sold many homes), we have stagers/designers help with making sure our money is well spent. A couple of bad design choices can cost you thousands, so make sure you are talking to your agent months in advance.

We are at the settlement table and our sellers spent $40K renovating the kitchen, as all the paperwork was getting signed. The seller playfully asked the buyer what their plans were for the house. The buyer, without skipping a beat, said they would remodel the kitchen as quickly as they could. Remember, when you are selling, it's not about what you want; it's about what the buyer wants. *I mentioned this story more than once because it happens more often then you think*

Last is pricing. Honestly, this is the easiest. If you have a great agent, they should be looking at where the market is, where the market was, and where the market is going. I see many sellers only focusing on homes that have sold and never taking the time to trend where the market is heading. In the end, it hurts and nets them less money in the long run.

Get with a knowledgeable agent and create a game plan, and you will win in the end.

THE RISK OF OVERPRICING YOUR HOME

Every seller wants the same thing. Mo' money, mo' money, and mo' money. Heck, when I sell my properties, I have the same feeling. Inevitably, I'll get the question, "Should I price my home higher, since the buyer is going to ask for a discount, so that I can eventually get my price?" The smarter sellers ask me the better question, "If I price my home high now, do I risk what I could get if I price it correctly at the beginning?" This is the best question I've ever been asked, and only 1 percent of sellers will ever ask it.

What most agents won't tell sellers is what they need to hear; we mostly default to what sellers want to hear. I say "we" because I've done it as well, mostly because we want to please you and make you feel good.

Anytime you gamble in Vegas, there's a risk that you may win or lose. The same risk is found when you gamble in real estate. Going for the "what if" price always comes at the risk of the sure price. Home buyers have more information now than they have ever had! They watch and follow homes and react like most folks would. If a home price drops or stays on the market longer because it's overpriced, they make the natural assumption, such as thinking something must be wrong with the house.

Negotiations in today's real estate world is all about perception, and you have one opportunity to shape that perception. I have always found that if you show right and price right from the first day you have a much higher likelihood of getting your price. You must fight the urge to gamble to get more because most of the time, the risk isn't worth the reward. I like the sure bets, especially when it comes to real estate.

I had a seller that could've gotten $735K if he had priced his home right at the beginning. He decided he wanted try to hit a home run at $830K. Five months later, that sure thing at $735K turned into a sure thing at $700K. The risk of trying to get $100K turned into losing $35K.

COMMISSIONS DON'T MATTER

We've all heard the quote, "You get what you pay for." In my life in real estate, I've found the value of having professionals surrounding me. My financial advisor, my mortgage lender, my real estate attorney and my accountant. They have all played a pivotal role in my success in real estate. They have all given me massive value, so much value that I don't even know what they charge me. In fact, I don't even desire to know. They all are fair, and I trust them with very valuable parts of my life. This leads me to commission. If you are buying or selling real estate and you are working with a true professional that's a master of their craft, they will make you far more money in real estate than they will ever charge you. You are essentially hiring an agent to represent you and your interest, and negotiate the best deal for you. If they can't negotiate their commission with you, how do you expect them to effectively negotiate with the market?

If you are an investor that is looking for deals to grow your real estate empire, you need agents to help you. If those agents know that you are focused on taking their money, then how can they focus on helping you make money?

Now, if an agent is not a good agent, then this point is moot. But if you have found someone that is one of the best at what they do, then that person will make you money or save you money—far more than you will ever pay them. Let them focus on that, and the relationship will pay you far more than you will ever save on discounting their commissions.

SELLERS: GET COMFORTABLE BEING UNCOMFORTABLE

- Buyers walking in and out of your home while you are getting ready for dinner.

- Buyers deciding your home isn't for them after it's been under contract for weeks, and you mentally considered it sold.

- Seller repairs that are supposed to be completed the day before the settlement, but aren't.

- Lender saying they have *all* of the paperwork needed, but come back at the final hour, needing one more document after you've packed everything to move.

- The mortgage rate you get quoted when you start shopping isn't the same rate when you get your home under contract.

- The contractor's quote goes up 10 percent by the time the project is completed.

These are just a few of the things that often happen in the world of real estate, and change is the only constant. Your success, longevity, and peace will be dictated by how you weather those changes that will surely come. I'd love to romanticize and tell you that the changes will sometimes be positive, but that rarely happens. It's likely a change that will require, at minimum, your time, mind space, and money.

The best way to handle these changing situations are to expect them, embrace them, and be proactive.

- **Expect it.** Ask your agent, contractors, and investors, "If something were to change or happen in this scenario, what would it likely be?" If they have enough experience, then they have likely been through this change or situation before. Ask them how they would recommend you respond and solve the problem if the same things happen to you.

- **Embrace it.** Most people run and hide from change. Don't do that! Step in front of it. It doesn't mean you have to like it, but a positive attitude will go a long way.

- **Be proactive** *after* you have done your homework, thought through the pros and cons, looked at the bigger picture, etc. Make quick, wise, and unemotional decisions. The person that's the most proactive generally controls the narrative.

THE FIRST OFFER IS THE BEST OFFER

Selling a home can be emotional. I mean, it's your home. You have owned it, invested in it, and lived in it. Those memories and emotions often cloud your decision making when the time comes to sell your home. Once you have made a decision to sell your home, you have to put on your logical lenses. Renovations, strategy, timing, and negotiations all require logic, but most sellers can't get out of their emotions to make the right decision for their long-term wealth.

If you prepare your home to sell properly and have a well thought-out strategy and marketing plan, then the best offer you get on your house will likely be the first offer. I've seen seller's receive a fair offer—sometimes a better than fair offer—and want to wait to see if they can get something better. In most cases, the cost of waiting and seeking more causes them the sure thing. That is when I find the emotions of the home interfere with your logic. I hear things like, "My home has this or that," or something "is bigger than or better than, so I should get this or that price." Believe me, I've been there and been stung by the same negotiating bug. Negotiating an offer to sell your home is all about leverage. The first offer has raised their hand, put pen to paper, written an EMD check and pictured what they are going to do with your home; this is the emotional leverage you need to get the best offer on your home. When you mix your emotions with the buyer's, you have simply leveled the playing field.

If you have made a decision to sell your home, the first offer should be taken seriously and negotiated seriously. While it may not be exactly what you want, it's likely the best opportunity to get what you need, which is your home sold.

Some things to think about:

- **The first person to fall in love with your home is likely the most serious buyer.** When other points of negotiation come like inspections, terms etc., they likely will be easier to work with.

- **The cost of holding a property should be calculated when selling.** What are your mortgage payments and other carrying costs associated with owning the property that will add up by waiting for a future offer?

- **Opportunity cost factors in greatly.** If you are buying more real estate after you sell (which you should be), what gains are you leaving on the table from the future home by waiting?

WHEN THE HIGHEST OFFER ISN'T THE BEST OFFER

Most people think that when selling their home, getting the *most* money is the signal of success. I can't lie, when I sit down with most sellers, I'm focusing on getting them top dollar as well. Our society unfortunately measures success monetarily first and other more important characteristics after that. There are times when that type of focus doesn't equal success in the long-term or even the short-term.

We recently had a client selling a really nice condo in DC. She did everything we told her to do, including staging and pricing correctly. After a week on the market, there were three offers, one with an escalation clause with no cap! (I wouldn't recommend this strategy.) The clause would make this offer the highest no matter what the other offers were. Seems like a no-brainer for the seller right? Not so fast!

The offer was a VA loan that would have likely taken longer to settle, which would've meant the owner would have two more mortgage payments and two more months of stress due to owning two places. The buyer on the other offer had more money in reserves. This was good because if any appraisal value issues came up, they had the margin to cover any differences.

After a few minutes of conversation, it was clear the higher offer wasn't the best offer for the seller.

If you are selling or even buying a home, you have to determine what is the most important factor to you and your overall success. If it's money, then so be it, but often with honest and open reflection, you will find that there are many other factors that matter to you.

If it's the house that you will be spending the next seven to 10 years in, then what does an extra $10K mean over the long run?

If you sell your home to the highest bidder, but they nitpick you to death at every inspection and are a nightmare to deal with for the next six weeks, how much is your peace of mind worth?

If you are selecting an agent that might cost you a bit more, but their track record of success is high. Is a couple of percentage points worth an expert's advice and guidance? Homes do matter and they are expensive.

If you hire the cheapest contractors, but they take weeks—I mean months—to finish, what is your time or stress level worth?

List your priorities of success and make sure your real estate decision is based *equally* on that set of criteria.

THE SILLIEST THINGS CAN KILL A
REAL ESTATE DEAL

"Common sense ain't so common these days." I'm sure you have heard this quote before. It speaks to all areas of life, but it yells in real estate. Imagine the mix of housing, money, emotions, family, agents, more money, repairs, negotiation, deadlines, contracts, etc. I can go on with more, but I think you get the point. With all these ingredients/factors going on at once, it creates an environment that's unpredictable. In that unpredictability, people let silly stuff derail an otherwise smart real estate deal.

This is a list of things that have killed a real estate deal:

- **A fridge:** The sellers were getting divorced, and the ex-husband found out the wife was getting the fridge. He previously thought the buyers were getting it. He refused to sign, knowing his ex-wife would be the benefactor of that shiny fridge!

- **A political sign:** Buyers saw a sign from a political party they didn't like and decided it wasn't the home for them.

- **Communication:** A divorcing husband and wife couldn't find a way to communicate in order to get the home sold. One wanted texts, the other wanted phone calls. The offer on the table walked away because they couldn't wait for them to figure it out.

- **A sofa:** A buyer bought a sofa the day of the settlement. The settlement ended up being delayed by two weeks, and that debt showed up on the credit report. The buyer couldn't qualify for the loan anymore.

- **Racism:** A buyer under contract parked in a neighbor's space. The neighbor came outside irate and said, "We don't like your kind here." Buyers didn't feel comfortable and walked away from the deal. This neighborhood is literally the United Nations, but one bad apple can spoil the bunch.

- **A job:** A buyer decided to take a new job the day before the settlement. He said he got a $5K raise and had to take the job. He lost the house and his $7K earnest money deposit. Changing jobs killed the deal as the lender could no longer fund the loan.

This list could go on and on! Just understand that this is the type of stuff agents have to navigate through every day. A good agent is worth their weight in gold. Pay them what they deserve. Be aware of the daily BS they deal with to make sure nothing kills your real estate deal!

THE ONE PERCENT RULE TO NEGOTIATING HOME INSPECTIONS PROPERLY

Most buyers and sellers focus primarily on the price they get for their home. They rarely focus on the importance of the condition of the home, and if they do, they have no strategy.

When negotiating the cost of any inspection items, we operate by the 1 percent rule. If you can get in or out of a home inspection for less than 1 percent of the sales price, then you are doing well. For example, if you're selling your home for $500K, and the buyer asks you for repairs that are less than $5K, then you're winning. If you're buying a home that costs $300K, and you get the seller to do $4,500 in repairs, then you have done a good job negotiating your inspection items.

There are always exceptions to any rule, but in general, this is the baseline that I use for home inspection costs.

No home is ever going to be perfect, and good inspections shouldn't only focus on issues.

Thirty-three percent of your inspection should find items that need repair, 33 percent should highlight any deferred maintenance issues, and 33 percent should focus on how your home works.

- **Items that need repairs:** Even brand-new homes have items that need repair. We have seen foundation issues, mold, and even structural issues in brand new homes. This doesn't mean these homes are bad; it just means that you can find repairable issues. Most homeowners don't even know about 90 percent of the issues until their inspector points them out. Rarely do we find items that can't be fixed, repaired, or replaced.

- **Maintenance issues:** These are items that aren't broken yet, but need to be serviced or maintained to make sure they stay in good, working condition. Most homeowners don't focus on these issues because most subscribe to the "if it ain't broke" mentality. We find that if you get ahead of these issues, then you could not only save yourself money, but also time and stress when something does break or is found in the inspection. These issues are much more costly to fix than they are to maintain.

- **How your home works:** This is the most important part of any inspection, and this is why we recommend buyers be present and alert at their inspections. It also helps to have a knowledgeable agent with you during this time. You will learn the inner workings of perhaps your most expensive investment ever. A baseline knowledge of heating/cooling, roof, structural, plumbing, and electric can help diagnose and avoid costly emergencies. Sometimes, it's the simple fixes that can save you a lot of time and money down the line.

SECRETS *AGENTS* USE WHEN THEY SELL THEIR OWN HOMES

These are a few of my seller tricks:

- **First impressions are everything!** Good agents will take the time to make sure every stone is turned. Even the small things matter to them, and even if it takes them an extra few days to get it right, they will. Cleaning carpets, changing lights, changing door knobs, replacing electrical plates, etc. They understand that it's not the major things that only need the focus; it's the small things.

- **Smart sellers are honest with themselves.** They ask friends if their home smells like animals or food odors. They ask other agents if their price is too high. They make those people feel very comfortable telling them things that they don't necessarily want to hear. They know that they'd rather hear it from friends than have the market tell them. They know that by the time the market tells them, it's too late.

- **Smart sellers price their home to sell within the first seven days.** They know that competition will likely yield the highest price! They never want their home to sit. Most of the time, pricing it a bit lower in the right market creates a frenzy. Frenzy when you are selling is a great thing.

- **Smart sellers always list on a Thursday evening.** Buyers getting ready to see homes on the weekend start compiling their list on Friday. If you're hot on the market on Thursday, then you'll have the buzz and energy from a fresh listing. Thursday also gives you enough time to create a possible multiple offer situation.

MASTERY OF THE BASICS OF REAL ESTATE

FINDING YOUR PERFECT PIECE OF REAL ESTATE

Imagine your perfect home! Whether it's a home for your family with the perfect backyard, that bachelor's pad with the fly balcony overlooking the city, or that cash flowing home that will be a perfect retirement play, all those properties are owned by someone that you likely do *not* know. Not only do you not know the person that owns them *yet*, but you also don't know when that person intends to sell it. This is why I tell my clients and friends to *always* be in the market for that *perfect* piece of real estate. That home of your dreams or investment of a lifetime rarely aligns with when you're ready to make a deal. It more than often comes when you're not ready and when you're not in the market.

I think back to when I met my wife. I wanted everything to be absolutely perfect before I proposed to her, but perfect timing and perfect money rarely align.

The same goes with real estate, your home or investment is never on your timeline; it's always on the seller's timeline. When a seller decides to retire, move up or move down, divest or simply move on to a bigger investment, they determine when that perfect property will be available for you to purchase.

A few tips to always be ready:

- **Pull an equity line off your properties as soon as you can.** You never know when you will run across a no-brainer deal that you wish you had money to buy.

- **Stay in your favorite agents' ears.** Have quarterly conversations with them. It lets them know that if they run across something they would buy, to let you know.

- **Keep your ears to the ground.** The best deal happens in the midst of a life-changing event, good or bad. Always ask if they have some real estate to sell.

- **Pick your partners early.** Some deals will require a partner. Getting your goals, structure, and lending in order early will allow you to pounce when you run across the right deal.

- **Always analyze and keep the property you own in sell-ready shape.** You never know when you will have to sell what you have in order to buy the place of your dreams.

YOU CAN'T TIME THE MARKET

In my career in real estate, I've seen up and down markets. The crash of 2008 was preceded by a robust real estate market a couple of years before. I've seen corrections, highs, lows, sellers' and buyers' markets, and everything in between. Through them all, there is money and success to be found in real estate. I'll say that again in a different way to make sure you understand: You can make money in up and down real estate markets. Timing the real estate market is nearly impossible. Sure, there are people that sold at the top of the market and bought at the bottom and made great money, but there are also investors that bought at the top of the market, held the property for 15 to 20 years, and made millions. Real estate, when played correctly and effectively, is a long game! Those that speculate on the real estate market are often subject to the decisions that others make around them. Most of the massively successful people, investors, developers, and clients have become lifelong real estate students. They understand long-term growth and investing for the future, instead of a paycheck right now. If you want to find massive success in real estate, let others play the short-term game, and you resolve to buy, hold, add value, and wait. In the end, you will win and have longevity in this game called real estate.

A couple of key things to think about:

- **When you buy and sell fast, you owe more taxes.**

- **Think long-term cash flow over quick flips.**

- **Imagine what an area or neighborhood could be in 20 years.** Invest in that now.

- **Stay away from the news.** By the time the news reports about real estate, the market has changed.

- **Hunker down in one area and resolve to understand everything about that area.**

- **Stay in your lane.** Don't hop all over the real estate asset class. Mastering one asset class will take you further than having some knowledge about all types of asset classes.

"Every adversity brings with it a seed of an equivalent advantage."
-Napoleon Hill, author of *Think and Grow Rich*

EXTRA AJ TIP:
In the world of investing, there will be less competition when the market is adjusting or dropping, but the same advantage to win will be there. You just have to adjust your strategy.

CHOOSING RELATIONSHIPS OVER SHORT-TERM GAINS

One of the principles that has served me well in real estate is understanding and playing the long game. I remember as a young investor and agent whenever something or someone did me wrong or what I perceived was wrong, I'd have to figure out a way to win. When a contractor overcharged me, a seller didn't do what I wanted them to do, a lender made a mistake, or a new home builder had a delay and needed more time; all these instances would mean war, and I had to win. When I look back on it, I did win! I would give them a piece of my mind, raise my voice, and make them concede. The problem was that I would often wreck a valuable *long-term* relationship for a *short-term* win. Short-term wins tend to backfire:

- The contractor that cost me an additional $400 would no longer call me back as quickly when I really needed him.

- The sellers no longer want to go the extra mile for my buyers because they view our relationship as war instead of a pleasant family buying their home.

- The lender that might refer me valuable people in my network is now more hesitant to do so.

- The new home builder rep is no longer throwing me small freebie upgrades.

As I've matured in this business I've learned that you can get more done with honey then hot sauce (I like hot sauce, but you get the point). Real estate and this world is smaller than you think. The way you treat people will always be remembered more than what you do for them. If you plan to be successful over the long-term, whether selling or buying a home, investing, or planning to make real estate a career, make a choice to think long-term in your relationships. Give *grace* and *build* relationships that will last, and you will find yourself on the winning side with friends (not foes) to share your victories with. What good is winning and not having good people to share it with?

GET CREDIT BEFORE YOU NEED CREDIT

Credit and money education unfortunately aren't taught as they should in our schools. Instead, schools teach history, shop class (I'm dating myself), or trigonometry. I never understood why one of the most capitalist countries in the world doesn't teach the "art" of money in grade, middle, and high schools. These are a couple of fundamental concepts that work universally when applied correctly:

- **Be a saver.** Make a decision to save more than you spend.

- **Live below your means.** Keeping up with the Joneses (or Kardashians for you millennials) will keep you living the life that you might not want to live. Be comfortable living with less now, so you can have the option to live with more later.

- **Have a fundamental understanding of credit and how it works, especially in the world of real estate.** Look at your credit report, study it, and ask questions about what makes your credit profile better or worse than in previous months or years. For example, I meet with real estate lenders often years before I made an investment, to make sure I was prepared.

- **Hire a great financial advisor and accountant and make sure they are real estate-centric.** It would be helpful for them to invest in real estate as well. These people should always help you make more money than they will cost you. Hire someone with whom you can have candid conversations and through whom you can filter important financial decisions.

EXTRA TIP:
Make sure they have money, I see so many people hire professionals that don't know how to manage their own affairs.

- **Pull equity lines off good real estate.** If you have significant equity in your primary home, get a HELOC, even if you don't need it right now. It's often the best source for cheap investment capital, and the interest is tax deductible.

EXTRA TIP:
If you're looking to start a business, get investment real estate, buy a home, or get *anything* that will involve you needing money from a lender, start *well* before you need it.

ALLEN JOHNSON

THE "C" WORD: COMMISSIONS, COMMISSIONS, COMMISSIONS

Here are some common questions that I am frequently asked:

- **How do real estate agents determine the amount of commission?**
  Commissions are based on the services you provide. If you
  provide full-service real estate representation, then you
  deserve and likely charge a higher commission. If you limit
  your services, then your commissions will likely reflect that.
  You will always get what you pay for.

- **Who pays the commission?** Sellers ultimately pay commission
  for both agents in the transaction. However, to be clear, the
  Buyer is responsible for paying their agent's commission. The
  way contracts are written, the buyer is actually providing their
  agent permission to ask the seller to pay his commission on
  your behalf for brokering the transaction. Buyers still need
  to understand that, even though the seller is paying the
  commission for their agent, the buyer is still hiring a realtor
  who is responsible for representing their best interest in one
  of the largest financial transactions of their life. Make sure to
  interview for the qualities that are important to you.

- **Can clients negotiate commission percentage?** What are the pros and cons of trying to do that? Yes, everything is negotiable, but you get what you pay for. There are four professionals that I never ask for a discount: my doctor, my lawyer, my financial advisor, and my real estate agent. One protects my life, the other keeps me out of court, and the last two make me money! A great agent is always worth double what you pay them in commission. An average agent is worth exactly what you pay them, and a bad agent will cost you money. Don't just look at the cost; make sure to measure the gain.

Some real life examples of getting what you pay for:

- Renovations that would have normally cost you $8K, now cost you $4K because your agent has relationships with contractors.

- The seller was going to do $12K worth of work to get the home ready for the market, but their agent's plan had them spending $8K, and the home still sold for top dollar.

- The agent negotiates a deal that nets the seller $5K more than expected.

- Home inspection repair items where most sellers would have fixed everything requested, were negotiated to a manageable and less costly list.

- After the sale, your agent refers you contractors that save you thousands because of their relationship with your agent.

There are many more examples of the true value versus cost of a great real estate agent. But the bottom line is that your agent gives you much more value then you calculate. Sometimes, we all need reminders.

The pros of negotiating are that you see what kind of agent you have before you hire them. If an agent will give their money back to you, imagine what they will do with your money. My rule of thumb is if you hire an agent and you are better at negotiating commissions than they are, maybe you need to find another agent. The cons are that you only have one time to make a first impression. You are hiring someone to represent you and the most important financial asset you have. Educated consumers place the most emphasis on performance and results, as a great realtor always makes you more money in the end.

THE YOUNG PERSON'S PLAN FOR REAL ESTATE WEALTH

Many of the strategies I used to build wealth in real estate weren't learned in school or through some great mentor; they were learned through common sense! In this world, I'm finding that common sense is becoming more and more of an asset. I bought my first place simply because it was the same amount as rent, and the FHA loan I used required very little money down. I moved into my townhouse and realized I wasn't really using my basement, so I decided to rent it out. After a few months, I realized I was saving more money, so I created a separate bank account to go buy another home. Within two years, I had enough to go buy a slightly bigger, nicer townhome, and I used the same formula. After six years, I owned three small, profitable investments and used very little of my own money to buy them! It's the perfect formula for young buyers to build real estate wealth. Use the fact that you can buy with very little money down and find a way to think outside the box.

The prototypical first-time buyer property is typically a great future investment property. Think about it: It's similar to the property you are already renting, and it would make the perfect investment property. I recommend to our younger clients to look at their first purchase as more of an investment than their permanent home. If and when they leave or relocate, now they turn their home into an investment rental.

Some will ask, "How long do you need to stay in one place to make buying a home worthwhile?" Rule of thumb is two years or more. If you buy with future investment in mind, how long you plan to stay won't matter; it will be a great income property after you move on.

Calculate how much you are paying in rent, how much you are paying in taxes especially with nothing to write off, and how much are you leaving on the table from market appreciation. Young buyers should always be looking to leverage a home with very little money down. That's the beauty and the opportunity of real estate! In a perfect world, they should be buying and moving every two years.

THREE VITAL LESSONS YOU SHOULD TEACH YOUR KIDS ABOUT REAL ESTATE

Much of my real estate success can be directly connected to my mother and father. While neither of my parents went to college, they taught me highly valuable life, business, and real estate lessons. They sacrificed so that I could have a more level playing field. I'm so grateful to them. They have created a real estate legacy that will outlive them, and this book is a perfect example.

I want to pass on some of the real estate lessons they taught me as a kid and young adult. Hopefully, these lessons will spark some interest in your child.

- **The difference between renting and owning:** This lesson is simple, so let your kids ask you questions about the difference between renting a home and owning a home, making sure you're prepared to answer.

- **The power of investing:** Years ago, my wife and I decided that we would buy a home to pay for each of our kid's college education. When it is time for them to graduate high school, we'll sell each home, which will have appreciated enough over time to cover the cost of their college educations. We've showed our kids these homes and told them why we bought them. It teaches them that we are willing to invest in them. We used a 15-year mortgage for each home, and we're using the rent payments to cover those mortgages.

- **The work that goes into investment properties:** I drive by work sites with my kids all the time to show them the work that goes into real estate investments. I don't want them to think that what they see on TV is what happens in real life or have the expectation that you can collect on an investment without putting in the work first.

IN THE END, IT WILL ALL MAKE SENSE

I've found in life, business, and real estate that the best advice or wisdom didn't feel like it at the time. In addition, things that really felt counter to my present moment, in the long run, ended up great for my long-term success.

We have practiced real estate at a high level through the best and the worst markets. I've delivered news about gaining thousands and losing thousands. The strength of success in any market, whether up or down, is having someone that will tell you what you need to know at that particular moment, which will eventually save you time, money, and stress.

It's easy to speculate up. When the market is going up, it doesn't take much skill or knowledge to help someone make a decision, but when a market is adjusting or settling down, speculating down is a completely different skill that only time, experience, and wisdom can navigate.

A couple of real-life examples:

- A seller is moving out of state, and wants to make a certain amount. Last year, that amount would have been no sweat. The current market is not what it was six months ago. (Yes, the real estate market moves that FAST!) The house that was worth $320K is now worth $300K. The seller cannot wrap his head around the change and ends up selling the same home he could've sold for $300K for $280K another six months later. Not only did he lose $40K, but he lost time and added stress.

- Another buyer wanted a very specific home, and since the market was coming down, they wanted to negotiate to get the lowest price possible (about $25K difference). After several months of back and forth, the builder finally got down to a price that made the buyer happy, but during the same time, the interest rate went up by a couple of points. The buyer ended up buying for $25K less, but with a payment that was a couple hundred more per month.

In both of these instances, I gave advice that didn't make them feel great at the time, but from experience, was the best advice for their long-term success. Don't get so caught up in your feelings that you can't process the wisdom that God is giving you. If you trust your agent and they have God's heart, in the end, it will work out for your good.

HIRING THE RIGHT PROFESSIONAL

HOW DO YOU *KNOW* WHEN YOU HAVE A GREAT AGENT?

These are qualities of a great agent:

- **They ask great questions.** These agents are continually probing and making sure they understand what you want and what you need. If you run across an agent that asks questions that make you think, probe, or re-examine, you likely are working with a great agent.

- **They don't work for commission.** They work for results whether it pays them now, pays them later, or pays them never. Great agents are willing to give you advice because real estate is just who they are. They live, love, and breathe it. They don't make decisions or give advice that is dictated by earning a commission check.

- **They invest in what they sell.** They understand the market so well that they invest in what they know and do. Great stock brokers own and invest in stock. Great agents own and invest in real estate.

- **They are constantly learning.** Ask your agent what was the last book they read or last conference they attended. The industry is constantly changing and evolving. Great agents are always seeking knowledge to share. The best question to test an agent's knowledge base: "How's the market right now?"

- **They are busy.** Busy agents won't always pick up the phone when you call. You might have to leave a message or call back. It's not because they don't like you or have time for you, but they are busy in the business of real estate. Their strength to you is they have a pulse on the market because they are constantly in the market. The experience and relationships from all the clients they are currently doing business with benefits all the future clients.

- **They are truthful.** Great agents won't tell you what you want to hear UNLESS its true. They won't mince words to make you feel better. They will tell you the truth, even if it makes you run off to work with someone else. They only know how to do business one way: the right way.

A GREAT AGENT IS YOUR BEST FRIEND

In the world of information at your fingertips, why isn't everyone rich in real estate? You can literally type any question and get an answer. There are experts in every topic of real estate on TV or teaching classes or writing books. Everybody and their mother has a real estate license these days. With all this abundance of information and access to knowledge, what separates those with real estate knowledge and those with real estate riches and success? The difference is as quoted in Napoleon Hill's *Think and Grow Rich*: "Knowledge will not attract money or any other kind of success, unless it is organized and intelligently directed, through practical plans of action, to a definite end of accumulating money."

It's the reason "Most professors have not amassed great wealth! They specialize in teaching knowledge, but don't specialize in the organization or use of knowledge for the accumulation of money." There are many people in real estate with whom you can choose to align yourself. If your goal is to simply do average in real estate, then hire an average agent. If your goal it to make real estate work for you at the highest level, then you align yourself with high-level professionals.

How do you know if you have found that person? Here's some advice:

- **Ask great questions.** I want to know not only if you sell real estate, but do you understand real estate "holistically." Do you understand how everything works? I don't want them to have all the answers, but I do want them to be well connected enough to know someone that does. Beware the agent with ALL the answers.

- **Do they own, operate, and invest in real estate?** Even if you are a homeowner that doesn't desire to be an investor, this type of agent is a valuable resource. You didn't buy a home to lose money; thus, it's an investment. This agent operates in that mindset and will help you protect that financial investment.

- **Build a relationship with this agent.** Refer them business, help them build relationships with other smart people you know. Don't be a taker! It's the quickest way to not get everything you can possibly get from this valuable relationship. Vendors, mentors, and partners that I work with and help me make money know that if I can go *out of my way* to help them financially, relationally, spiritually, or in business, I will. Thus, when I call, I have their full attention.

- **What do other agents think about them?** Ask other agents about them. Reputation and character in your workplace and among peers will tell you a lot about that agent. Try to find the agent's agent.

YOU HIRE ME TO HELP
YOU MAKE DECISIONS

Consider the following:

- **Knowledge:** Everyone has access to information these days. My dad's favorite phrase is if you don't know something, then just simply "Google it." I laugh when he says this because he is the smartest and wisest real estate mind I know, and he never had Google. With all the books, podcasts, and seminars out there on any and all the subjects related to real estate, why are so many people lacking knowledge in this business of real estate?

- **Understanding:** The reason many don't thrive is because they have access to the knowledge, but they lack understanding. They can pass the test, but can't understand how it applies in real-world situations. Understanding comes from taking the knowledge and peeling the onion back. It requires seeking mentors, listening to stories, and reviewing the knowledge while doing the action. I find that many folks will read the information once or twice and never revisit or review what they learned. They never understand the information well enough to use it.

- **Wisdom:** This is the final step and very rare. Taking the knowledge and understanding, and knowing when, where, how, and with whom to use it. That's called wisdom. It's found at the crossroads of time, patience, setbacks/challenges, humility, and courage. It's when you operate off instinct, experience, and faith.

THERE ARE NO REAL ESTATE SCHOOLS
FOR REAL ESTATE AGENTS

If you only knew the level of education, competence, and overall common sense in the real estate industry, it would scare you. No wonder people feel comfortable trying to do it on their own. No wonder the Zillows and Redfins of the world are trying to eliminate the role of the agent. I think the fundamental reason is that real estate agents don't focus on the importance of continuous learning and education.

I speak to and mentor many kids, and I hear more and more often that they don't think they need to go to college anymore. They can bypass the four-year college and the debt that comes with it for cheaper options like going straight into the workforce, community college, getting certifications, or starting their own business. They often state that since they don't know what they really want to do, why should they waste money on college? I advise that while that might work for a small minority, the most important thing about going to college is "to learn *how* you learn." That's a vital skill that takes time to figure out in life, and it took me most of four—well, actually five—years to figure it out. (I was a super senior!)

This gets back to the area that most real estate agents never figure out. Learning, growing, and mastering your craft is on you! It's not opening doors to homes or standing at an open house. It's not the sexy, glamorous life you see on HGTV or Bravo. It's the dirty work that most agents aren't willing to do and don't even know how to do.

Think about it: A great athlete spends two to three hours every day honing their craft. Someone dedicated to their health works out one hour every day. But most agents are only required 8 to 16 credit hours (the equivalent of two to three hours per year) to maintain their license.

Agents in most states are only required to take one course to become a licensed, practicing agent. If you own a home and depend on someone to help you sell a $250K asset (which is about the average home price in the U.S.), this should scare and concern you.

Now, there are freaking phenomenal agents that have PhD-level real estate education. Most of the relevant knowledge needed to be a great agent isn't learned in a classroom setting.

These are the areas that you need to focus on when it comes to hiring a great agent or becoming a great agent:

- **Local market knowledge:** Knowing neighborhoods, schools, communities, upcoming development, traffic patterns

- **Investment knowledge:** Understanding the fundamentals of a money: lending, ROI, cash-on-cash return, basic real estate investing

- **Home construction:** Base-level knowledge of vital systems, network of contractors, understanding the building process and base-level costs of home repairs.

- **Negotiation:** Interpersonal skills, risk and opportunity assessment, leverage tactics

- **Ethics and integrity:** Trustworthiness and logic

There are more areas that are important to being or hiring a thorough real estate beast! Understand that this agent can either make you money, lose your money, or protect your money. Therefore, make sure their skillset reflects the level of service you need.

WHAT WE GET PAID DOESN'T MATTER

Let's get one of the most talked-about issues in real estate straight: commission!

I'm a highly productive agent and a highly productive owner of real estate, so I've seen and been affected by both sides of the commission coin.

As an agent, I get the question (mostly from people that either don't understand money or don't make a lot of money) about reducing my commission standard. The first thing those folks don't understand is that commission is split between two entities, the buyer's agent and seller's agent. Let's use 6% as the "common" commission rate in this scenario (side note—there is no industry standard commission rate. This would be called price fixing which is illegal in most industries). So when they are talking about the commission that their agent makes, it's likely 3 percent, not 6 percent. Now, from that 3 percent, agents have to pay out three times. Their brokerage (1/2 percent), their marketing (1/2 percent), and Uncle Sam/taxes (1 percent). So in most cases, their agent is controlling 1 percent, and that covers their expenses and their income. Now, if a seller asks for a discount in commission, which area do you think their agent has to pull the discount from? Uncle Sam? Try it if you like. Their brokerage? Not a chance. This leaves their income and, most important to you if you're selling, your marketing budget for your home. I'm a firm believer that if you market a product correctly, then you have a better chance of selling it *and* selling it for a higher profit. This leads me to what smart sellers and savvy consumers focus on: their bottom line. People with smart money IQ focus on what they will NET more than what their agent will make. They couldn't care less what commission they are charged (within reason) if they are going to walk away with the check they want. They refuse to focus on what the agents are making as long as they net what they are expecting. A great agent is supposed to make you money. A great agent is supposed to mitigate your real estate risk. A great agent is always worth way more than you pay them. If you feel the need to reduce your agent's commission, then you likely don't have a great agent.

Now, from the investor's side of the table: I've purchased and sold many homes that I have not represented myself. I've ALWAYS paid agents exactly what they are worth. I'm never shortsighted on the economics or the long-term relationship. If I want more deals, then I want to make sure that agent knows that I want them to make money. The number one mistake I see most investors make is focusing on commission more than the deal. I couldn't care less if that agent makes $10K or 4 percent if the deal is worth much more. Some of my best and most lucrative deals are from agents that got paid on both sides of the deal. I never ask for a reduction or even care. If the deal is great, then they deserve everything they make and more.

Investors and sellers, choose your focus wisely.

JACK OF ALL TRADES AND MASTER OF NONE

Would you go to a corporate attorney to handle your landlord issue? Would you go to a foot doctor to handle a skin issue? No, that would make no sense.

I run across agents with cards that say they cover multiple areas and multiple types of real estate. Our area is called the DMV. Washington, DC, Virginia, and Maryland are all within 10 miles of each other. It makes sense for a real estate professional, real estate lawyer, and contractors to want to cover all areas. The areas are geographically close enough, but contractually, the difference in markets are very different. These differences leave a lot to think about:

- **Let's start with the contract.** Each state and sometimes each county has contracts that are very different. If you miss a clause or timeline, or don't write or execute a contract correctly, you could leave money on the table and risk thousands for the client you represent.

- **The next thing to think about is the market.** You can drive 10 miles in any direction and have completely different market factors, trends, and strategies. I personally own properties in each market and see the distinct differences in each location. One street, one block, or one school zone can make a significant difference in market value of a piece of real estate.

- **What about the agent that says he sells residential, commercial, and investments?** There's a difference between *can sell* and *sells it well*. I've found that when you get into different types of real estate, you need a specialist! I even have a commercial agent that I hire to guide me through that process. Now that doesn't mean I'm not smarter than most due to my experience, but what that does mean is I know enough to know I don't know enough!

- **Contractors can work in several different areas, but I've found that there are specific factors that are commonly found in certain areas.** I try to find a contractor that has enough experience to know those factors and shorten my learning curve and thus save me money, time, and frustration.

A couple of questions to ask:

- Is this an area you specialize in?

- What trends or factors are you seeing in this particular area that I need to be aware of?

- Is there someone you know, that might be more experienced in this area or subject matter that you can refer me to?

YOU'RE BEING UNREASONABLE

Buying, selling, or investing in real estate is about money, no doubt. Can you make money off this deal? Are you losing money when you sell or buy? Is the rent coming in on time? Why is the buyer asking for so many repairs? You get the idea. When large sums of money are involved, emotions and reason become involved as well. Often, emotions and reason move erratically with the ebb and flow of money. I've been there.

AJ REAL-LIFE EXAMPLE:
Here's a recent example of evicting a non-paying tenant. He had only been in the house for six months and lost his job. He moved from another state and brought his family for a new start with the new job. He let me know when he lost his job that they would have to move back home because he could no longer afford the rent. My first reaction was emotional and saying those things would've only made a bad situation worse. When dealing with someone leaving your rental property, there's bad, and there's worse. Not paying and leaving the home in bad condition when you leave is a double whammy. Not paying and leaving the home in good condition for the next tenant it optimal. I quickly got out of my emotions and used

more reason and logic. By God's grace, he left the place in reasonable condition, so the next tenant could quickly move in and start making up for lost rental income. I still took him to court for lost rental income and some minor damage, but it could have been much worse. As a young landlord, I would have no doubt been emotional and perhaps made the situation worse.

When you are making decisions on money and real estate, give permission to your agent or trusted advisor to tell you if you're being emotional or not acting with reason. It's tough to recognize it when you're in the middle of negotiating or handling a tenant issue.

Also understand the other people involved may be acting in emotion and without reason, and you need to sometimes give them space and grace to get out of their feelings.

Sound real estate decisions and investments are made when your mind is clear and you have people around you that can help you get centered.

REAL ESTATE AIN'T SEXY

What you see on HGTV or BRAVO isn't the reality of everyday real estate. We operate in the world of REALITY: real-life homes with real-life people with real-life challenges. Tenants lose their jobs. Pipes burst when you leave for vacation. Buyers back out on deals. Sellers cover up things they don't want you to see. The home you want costs more than you can afford. HVACs typically break down when you need them the most.

If you decide to invest in real estate, buy a home, or sell a home, embrace the good, the bad, and the ugly. Accept that there will be challenges. Just because difficulties may arise, there is no need to run for cover. Remember this too shall pass. It's the reason I only hire and work with people that have been through challenges in life. They have proven to me that they can conquer or sometimes simply outlast or outsmart a challenge. When you are thinking about partnering or hiring someone to do this thing called real estate, ask them if they have ever failed in real estate? Don't judge them by their failure, but instead ask what did they learn and how did they bounce back? I've earned a PhD in working through some real estate challenges; they have benefited me, my family, and team in the long run. They have certainly benefited our clients and investors.

If someone is telling you a real estate story, and it seems too good to be true, it likely is. Unless they can give you multiple examples of how they

---

ALLEN JOHNSON

failed their way forward to reach the success they have accumulated. Be sure the professional you hire or the advisor who has your ear actually says something that speaks to their decision making, character, or business acumen. In my experience, every success story has a beginning, middle, and end.

Real estate is a grind, a long play, but on the other side, it's a beautiful, smart play. As my dad always says, "People always need food and shelter, and as far as I've seen, they ain't making any more land."

I CAN'T SAVE YOU

Former clients hired me to help buy and kinda sell their home (I'll explain the "kinda" shortly). We'd been talking housing and real estate for four years or more. The older couple was downsizing and were kicking around options that involved decreasing the size of their home and size of their monthly mortgage payment.

My suggestion was to do it sooner rather than later, because I felt the market was shifting toward one that would net them less money later. Several years later, I got a call that they were ready to rock, and I could sense a bit of panic and some desperation. I learned that one of them lost a job, and now they were living on one income. As predicted, the market now was different, and they lost a significant amount of equity. They were also counting pennies and wanted me to reduce my commission to help make up for the equity they'd lost. I made a business decision not to do that, and they decided to buy a home with us and sell with a different agent. Several months later after the home didn't sell and they'd lost even more equity, we had a conversation about what went wrong. I told them, "I can save you from a lot of things: inspections, predictable pitfalls, contractors, bad agents and negotiations, but I can't save you from yourself. If you choose to make bad decisions, there's no amount of skill I can employ."

I've been blessed, and I believe our clients have been blessed as well. We study the market and take our craft seriously. In fact, one of our core values is "master your craft." My father raised me to be a man that will tell you straight, mostly with grace, but also with honesty, whether you want to hear it or not. It always comes from a place that will look to the future, while recognizing and navigating the present realities. It's not always what you want to hear, but it's what you *need* to hear. We have saved many people through real estate. The one thing or person we can't save you from is yourself. Don't hire or engage with a professional if you are not going listen or do what's needed to make the best decisions. There are plenty of agents that don't take this profession seriously and will let you do anything you want to do, whether it's good for you or not.

WHY YOUR AGENT LIES TO YOU

I know this is a touchy subject, but let's get this out in the open: You're lying if you say that you've never lied! I'll bet that if you're honest with yourself, you have lied recently! I know I have.

I still tell my girls that Santa and the tooth fairy are real. I do it because I don't want to steal their joy and wonder. It's the same reason why your agent might lie to you. I'm not saying that *all* agents lie, but I am saying that there are so many moving parts in real estate, that it's easy to gloss over something that's not important to getting you to your end goal.

Recently, my seven-year-old daughter was doing something she knew she had no business doing. In the classic parent-kid scenario, I asked her what she was doing, and she said—you guessed it, "Nothing Daddy." Now, I saw her doing it, and it wasn't nothing. It wasn't a big deal nor was it serious until she decided to lie about it. I asked her if she was lying to me, and she doubled down on the first lie. You can think back to your childhood days about how the rest went down, but it illustrates how easily the truth gets bent. In an instant, nothing becomes something because we decide not to pause and admit when something is going wrong.

Most—99 percent of the time—in real estate, the mistake is not on the agent, but agents often want to protect your feelings and tell you what you want to hear at the time instead of what you need to hear.

Many years back, I was selling a house during a hot market. We put the home on the market on a Thursday (which is the best day to list your home, by the way), and by Sunday, we had three really good offers on the table. The seller decided to go with one of the offers on Monday, but with the continued activity, asked me, "Allen, did I get any more offers on my house, and if I did, would you tell me about them?"

Now, the agent in me wanted to say "no" because if he did get offers, then it would lead to more discussions, more time, more dealing with offers and agents, etc.

But the truth was that he did get more offers that I didn't want tell him about because they were much lower than the ones he had on the table.

I told him, "Yes, you have more offers, but I figured that you wanted to focus on the one that netted you $30K more."

He said, "Yeah, because my neighbor said his friend wrote an offer, and I wondered if that was it. Thanks for keeping me focused on making the most money. My family and I need it for our next house."

Now I'll admit, everything in me wanted to lie and make it easy for myself. But in business, real estate, and life, those little lies won't all catch up with you, but one will.

 AJ True Story: The Williams Story
The seller was relocating out of town. I met with them, and the house was decent, but not great. The seller took my advice and decided to wait 30 days to rehash the conversation. They called me back saying they were ready to sell and wanted me to come back by the home. Now I'd already seen it before, but they insisted. This home and the level of detail they put into

getting it ready for the market was remarkable as was the reason they wanted me to see it. I've remodeled, staged, and been in many homes, and this job was in the top three of my career. They literally did everything I told them and more.

We went to the market, and within two months, we had a contract. They moved to their new place and waited for the settlement. On a random Sunday (it's always a Sunday or vacation), the buyer's agent called me and shared bad news. The buyer didn't qualify for the loan, based on blah, blah, blah! I say blah, blah, blah because I've heard it all before and seen deals work out and deals fall out. This agent wanted my seller to contribute more money toward the deal in order to get it closed. Being in this business for a while, I knew that contribution could come from anyone, and I didn't feel my clients should bear the burden of that mistake, but I also knew that if we had to wait another two months for a contract, that would cost my seller something as well.

I pulled a tactic from Dale Carnegie's classic book *How to Win Friends and Influence People* and put the praise and responsibility back on the agent and buyer. By the grace of God and experienced negotiating, we got the deal closed.

Now the lie! During this entire time, the seller was calling from out of town asking me if everything was going alright. And I will admit that I lied. I told them everything was going great and that everything was on track for the settlement. In hindsight, I shouldn't have done that, but the reason I didn't was that I wanted to protect them, and I didn't want them to worry.

Your agent will most likely not lie to you because they want to hide the truth from you. They most likely would lie to keep you focused on what's best for you. Either way, it is wrong.

TACKLING RENOVATIONS & REPAIRS

QUALITY MATTERS

In this world of easy buttons, quick fixes, and finger-tip experts, there are a couple of things you can't do easily: produce quality and gain experience. In the world of real estate, those two things will make you wealthy and help you weather storms and challenges that will surely come.

AJ TRUE STORY:
A client decided to paint his house, but he decided to buy a slightly cheaper quality of paint, trying to save a little money. When it came time to sell the home, the cheaper quality of paint wouldn't allow the seller to wipe various spots on the wall down. Instead, the seller had to repaint walls, which costed him two times more than simply buying a better quality paint from the start.

AJ TRUE STORY:
A client decided to use a discount agent and save on commission when buying a new home. The inexperienced buyer made all the decisions and guided their own negotiations and decisions. One decision was to not add a second parking space in a condo community that lacked adequate parking. When the homeowner decided to sell the condo, their value dropped by $40K, based on a parking space that originally cost $15K. Since the agent lacked the experience necessary and offered limited services and attention to detail, the 2 percent in commission savings cost the seller three times more money when they eventually sold the home.

Over my 17 years of owning and selling real estate, I too, have been burned by trying to cut a corner or save a buck—many more times than I'd like to admit. I find it mostly with my investment properties. Repairs and renovations that I could have spent a little extra time fixing, addressing, or upgrading always creep back up at the least opportune time, like when I'm on vacation, on a weekend, or out with family.

In the world of real estate, you will eventually get what you pay for. You can pay a little more now and get quality and expertise, or you will pay much more later. As the old folks say, "It will all come out in the wash."

ALLEN JOHNSON

MRS. AND MR. DO-IT-YOURSELF-ER

I love and respect handy homeowners. It's a skill that is actually a lost art in my opinion. It is something that I think you can actually make big money at if you packaged and sold it right. The reason "Mrs. *and* Mr." are in my title is because my wife is the one in our family most likely to turn a wrench correctly. And I love it.

There's a big difference between fixing an issue like a running toilet, garbage disposal, or loose rail versus doing a renovation. With the rise of HGTV and other channels that highlight renovations and fixer-uppers, we are seeing more and more unqualified homeowners diving into projects that might save them money up front, but cost them more in the end.

I visited a seller recently that was getting ready to put their home on the market. It was a nice home in a higher price point for the area. They painted all the kids' rooms in a nice color, but the trim and ceiling lines weren't done correctly. She went on to tell me she took three days off from work to paint them. While emotionally I'm sure it was fulfilling, they ended up paying more in the end (three days off from work plus getting professional painters equals more than getting the professional painters from the beginning).

I can tell you hundreds of similar stories about tiling flooring, cabinets, trim work, windows, etc., done incorrectly.

The bottom line is if you can't do it to professional quality, then understand when it comes time to sell, you will likely have to have it done again. And that "again" will likely cost you more than paying someone to do it right the first time. That said:

- If you are handy and really good at it, then this doesn't apply to you.

- If you are fixing something that is cosmetic and likely won't affect your home value, then this doesn't apply to you.

- If you just want the satisfaction of turning a wrench or find peace in fixing things, you are welcome to come over to my properties and find some peace.

However, if you are a homeowner that is concerned about your bottom line and netting every dollar from your home, hire a professional the first time, get it done right, and choose wisely what and where you spend your time and money.

As the old folks say, it all comes out in the wash.

RENOVATING TO SELL VS. RENOVATING TO RENT

When you sell a home, you are looking to get the maximum price for the home. What most property managers and agents don't tell their clients is the cost or investment of your renovations likely won't equal the value you will get out when you sell. In fact, that number gets even more out of control when you renovate to rent.

For example, if you are renovating to sell and rip out a kitchen, it may cost you $50K. There's no guarantee that you will get $50K more for your home. In fact, in most cases, you would net more money pricing the home $40K less and selling the home to a buyer who will renovate themselves.

AJ TRUE STORY:
I had a client that gutted her master bath a few months before she sold her home (against my advice)—brand new everything that cost her $25k. At the settlement table (back in the day when buyers and sellers were in the same room), I ask the buyers what was the first thing they were going to do when they moved in. Without missing a beat, she said, "Remodeling the master bathroom to get the tub I always wanted!"

When renovating to rent, you may spend $25K painting, flooring, and sprucing the bathrooms up to get ready to rent the home. Those renovations will only get you $200 more per month in rent. It will take you 10 years to get your renovation money back! In 10 years, styles change, renters leave wear and tear, and you still are likely to have to renovate again when you prepare to sell.

These examples are true stories that I've seen many times throughout my career. Most real estate professionals and property managers are good at selling, buying, or renting, but not at high-level strategy. Thus, you must be the steward of how to spend your money wisely.

Basic rules of thumb when developing your renovation strategy:

- **Start early if planning to sell.** If you're renovating to enjoy your home, then do it when you can enjoy it. If any major renovation that is happening within 18 months prior to selling your home, understand that you are risking netting less than you expect.

- **Do cost analysis.** If you are renovating to rent a home, do a cost analysis before you do any major renovations. Look at area rental comps carefully and calculate how long it will take you to recoup your investment. If it's any more than three to five years, then it might not be the best investment of your money or time.

- **Wait on any major renovations for rental properties.** With investment properties, you are likely to have to renovate just before you sell your home. There are some instances where you can net what you invest and maybe more. The key is to make sure you handle any repairs needed to maintain that rental, but save your renovations for when you hit the market.

These don't include repairs and preventative maintenance; those should always be done as soon as possible!

HOW TO PICK A GOOD, RELIABLE CONTRACTOR

First of all, let me debunk this myth! There's no such thing as a 100 percent good and reliable contractor. The days of a great handyman or general contractors are gone. Realize that most new homes are built in factories by machines, and the skills of a handyman of the past aren't taught in schools anymore. Everyone specializes in something these days, which has made it harder to find a good, reliable contractor that can help the average homeowner.

There are a couple of tricks that I've used over the past 20 years that have helped me find the right people for my real estate journey.

- The first and most effective way is word of mouth. Ask friends who they used and if they were happy with them.

- Ask the seasoned professionals at your local Home Depot, Lowe's, or Ace Hardware who they'd recommend. They see contractors all the time and can quickly identify the good and bad.

- Ask your agent who they use. If your agent is in the business of real estate, they should have some contractors worthy of an honest estimate and quality job.

- Drive by your local new home site. They are littered with contractors that might want to make a little extra money on the side with a quick job. Keep in mind they are normally bigger companies, so your job might be too small, but good guys often do work on the side.

- Renovation job sites are another good place to find a few good contractors. I often stop my car and walk on job sites that aren't mine, especially if they are local, and survey the work, ask questions, and get cards or phone numbers for future work.

If you do these things, you will find a few good options for future work that your home or investment might need. Also keep in mind a few things: Relationships take time. Build that relationship with your contractors; they may not be perfect or 100 percent reliable, but over time, they will save you stress, time, money, and most of all, help you protect your investment.

PROTECTING YOUR INVESTMENT/LANDLORD 101

THE PERFECT RENTAL PROPERTY

There are many ways to buy and manage rental properties. I'm often asked, "Should I buy a rental?" "How can I buy a rental?" or "Where should I buy my rental?" Here is a list of the things I like to look for in my perfect rental property:

- **Location:** I like locations close to my home. At first, I didn't understand the importance of distance, but with age, time is becoming more and more important. When emergencies happen, they rarely happen on your timeline, so being close helps you not have to spend precious time dealing with the problem and rearranging your schedule to get there.

- **Workforce housing:** Rentals for people that are in the normal workforce have always worked well for me. Middle class folks that work a regular nine-to-five job are always going to be a strong rental pool to pick from. They generally take good care of your property and don't expect costly upgrades.

- **Townhouses over condos/single family homes:** Townhouses have been the perfect rentals for me. Condos do have less maintenance, but they also have higher fees, which eats into monthly cash flow. Single family homes generally don't have fees, but they do have more maintenance. Townhouses are the perfect rental mix. They are big enough to accommodate larger families, but small enough to not have the maintenance of a single family home. Remember, the bigger the property, the more it will cost to upkeep, renovate, and repair.

- **Kinda fixer-uppers:** I say "kinda," because I don't want to buy a rental that needs a FULL overhaul. I normally go for fixer-uppers that need some updating. I like the sweat equity it builds for the future and the additional cash flow it generates, due to the upgrades. The reason I don't like full renovations is the length of time it takes to get the rental ready for the market and cash flowing. The quicker you can turn the property, the faster you can move on to the next. Think cosmetic, carpet, paint, flooring, tile, etc.

ALLEN JOHNSON

SHOULD I RENT OR SELL MY HOME?

I get this question quite often. I think since I'm an investor and own rental properties, everyone expects me to say you should rent it. On the flipside, because I'm an agent, other clients might think that since I get paid to sell homes, I'd advise to sell it.

Every situation is different, and in every situation, I need all the facts to give my appropriate recommendation.

I recently went on a listing appointment, and the first thing I noticed were fans. Fans were everywhere, and it was hot! I mean really hot. Now I'm warm blooded and actually prefer the heat, but even I was uncomfortable. During my consultation, the seller told me the HVAC had been out the entire summer, and she couldn't afford to fix it. Her next statement to me was, "I'm thinking I should rent this home instead of selling it."

What do you think I told her?

If you can't afford to fix the cooling unit now, what is going to happen when you're responsible for renters as a landlord? As a homeowner, you can choose to not have it working. As a landlord, you're contractually obligated to keep everything working.

I can tell you many similar situations.

These are a few basic rules/questions to ask yourself to determine whether you should rent your home or sell it:

- Are you planning on EVER moving back in the home?

- Do you have the patience or desire to be a landlord?

- Does the property have cash flow?

- Do you have six months of mortgage and emergency repair reserves?

- Do you have access to a reliable property manager? (This is the toughest job in our industry.)

- Where is the current real estate market?

- What type of tenant are you likely to attract?

- If you sell, what will you do with the money?

- What are the tax implications for selling vs. buying?

Remember, just because you think you want to be a landlord doesn't mean it's the best financial decision. Find a real estate professional that will walk you through the benefit analysis above. Trust their guidance and judgment. I've seen many clients make bad "rent vs. sell" decisions, and it ended up costing them in the long run.

TIPS FOR TURNING OVER YOUR RENTAL PROPERTY

This is the sexy side of real estate investing. You know the side that is captured in 30-minute segments on HGTV? Not! I've heard it said that success isn't sexy. It's often found in the boring, day-after-day, year-after-year tasks that most don't want to do.

You have heard me talk about my real estate retirement plan, $50K in cash flow per month from paid-off real estate. For that to happen, I've estimated that I will have to interact personally or through a property management company with over 1,000 tenants. Thus, having a strategy around dealing, and specifically turning, my rentals properties over with less money and stress is essential to my retirement goal.

Now let me warn you, even the best-laid plans are subject to jerks, scumbags, and bad tenants. This is part of the game that makes most people not want to get into rental investment property. The most successful investors know this is not desired, but is expected, and they put a game plan together to avoid what can be avoided.

Here are a couple of things to think about for your retirement rentals:

- **They are your investments.** You need to treat them for long-term appreciation. This is a mindset shift.

- **Try to get your rental on a spring/summer cycle.** If you are entering a lease during the winter months, talk to the tenant about extending to the spring or early summer. You are the landlord, so you get to set the rules up front.

- **Price it to rent FAST.** A vacant property for a couple of months will cost you money. Do the math. An increased competition gets you the choice of the best tenants.

- **Plan for any capital improvements during the turnover time.** Those improvements include windows, roof, heating/cooling, hot water heater, etc.

- **Communicate your expectations of your tenant a few months before they move out, so there is no confusion.** I like to highlight the portions of the lease and send it to them 45 to 60 days before they move out.

These are a few things that have helped me. Remember, if you are in this game, you *will* run across some challenges, but long-term, when it's all said and done, those properties will allow you to live a lifestyle that most could only wish for.

PREVENTIVE MAINTENANCE ON A RENTAL PROPERTY

We have discussed that rental properties are different and should be treated differently than your primary residence. The one thing I've noticed over my years of owning investment real estate is that renter's always live *harder* in homes. What would not break in your home will in a rental. Things that worked just fine when you lived in the home now seem to break on the regular.

The true cost of owning a rental property is not only found in the cost to repair these items and issues, but in the stress and time it takes to handle them. There are a few strategies that I've found useful in limiting some of these issues.

WARNING:
If you are planning to do this real estate investing *for real*, you can't eliminate everything, but you can handle some things. If you can forecast and remove 50 percent of your rental issues before they happen, this book and this page alone with be well worth the investment in knowledge.

- **Take all washers and dryers out of rentals.** They get the most use and tend to break. If you can get the tenant to purchase their own, then you eliminate the maintenance calls that are likely to come. The key is the make sure they install them properly. Write a clause in your lease that they have to be professionally installed with the appropriate receipt.

- **Take out all garbage disposals.** Again, these are the most likely appliances to break, leak, or get clogged. Most tenants tend to put any and everything thing down the sink. They actually think the name is true! Thus, you will get calls about things where common sense should've prevailed, but didn't (potato skins, chicken bones, plastics, etc.). Just taking this out of the home will save you at least two calls.

- **Remove ceiling fans.** These are nice to look at, but are often the small service calls that can be avoided and don't offer any extra value to your rental price. Put a nice dome light instead and save yourself the expense of needed an electrician to fix it.

- **Service HVAC (spring and fall).** This will save you those calls that can't wait. The emergency calls when you are getting on the plane to enjoy your vacation. When these units break, they never do at a convenient time; it's always an emergency and needs to be handled quickly. If you put a service plan on your heating and cooling, and have a professional look, clean, and diagnose it biannually, you will save yourself stress and actually enjoy the vacation that rental property afforded you.

IT'S ALL GOOD UNTIL IT'S NOT

I've found that it's not good to be friends with your tenant. You can, by all means, be friendly and cordial, but it's best to do this without entering an actual friendship with them. The danger of being overly friendly with your tenant comes when there's a problem. The choice becomes difficult and personal: Do I protect my real estate asset or my friendship? Here are a couple of things to think about as you manage your investment rental.

- **Never, ever rent to family.** I've seen many rental situations involving family, and they NEVER turn out well.

- **Understand your lease and live by it.** There will come a time when you will pull that lease out to enforce a rule that the tenant violated. You want to make sure they can't bring anything up that you did wrong. Always err on the side of doing the right thing, even if they don't notice.

- **Always document.** It's easy to document these days through text, email, and letters. This allows you to document every conversation.

- **Never rent to someone that is difficult during the application process.** It will only get worse during the lease period.

- **Whenever you have repairs, give your handyman permission to snap a few pictures of how the tenant is living.** This may save you from having to go over and inspect the property every month.

- **Add a repair service deposit to the lease.** We put it at $100 for every call. This must be enforced wisely, but it can keep you from having a needy tenant, needing any and everything fixed. Use your common sense with this. If this is something you should have fixed or is your responsibility, then don't enforce it.

- **Make friends with the neighbors.** When I renovate, I like to know the neighbors. They will alert you to anything that needs your attention. Don't be a snitch and go throw the neighbor under the bus, but it may signal it's time for a pop-up visit.

- **Fix everything correctly the first time.** Just because it's a rental and you don't live there, doesn't mean you shouldn't treat it like your own home. Repairs and emergencies never come when it's convenient for you to fix them. Handle it up front and save yourself the stress.

EXTRA AJ TIP:
Never put your home address on your lease for ANY reason. Get a PO Box.

GIVE GRACE

When I was young, I thought like a young man. The world was mine, and it all revolved around me. As I've gotten older in life and real estate, my thoughts are wiser, and discernment has been earned. I remember when working with contractors, I'd wrestle and negotiate to the last dollar, and then and only then would I feel like I'd won. Or when negotiating a real estate contract, if I didn't get everything I wanted, I wouldn't feel like I was at my best or did my job. Perfection was the goal, and if I didn't reach that bar, there was still work to do. If I'm completely honest with you, I lost relationships, lost sleep, and lost the essence of doing good business. I remember having a talk with my dad and him sharing something so simple that changed all of my relationships personally and in real estate. He said, "Treat your relationship and contractors the way you would want to be treated. You can't hold people to perfection."

That statement changed the way I treated my clients, contractors, investors, and partners. I was getting frustrated with people not thinking about the long-term implications. I remember ending a contractor relationship over $4K. If I'd thought a little about it, this contractor helped me on projects that would've made that $4K look like lunch money. I remember haggling over a contract with a seller that ended up having several other properties that I would've loved to buy.

I remember holding a hard stance over $150 with a tenant; that stance soured a relationship that could have been easily fixed. That tenant moved out and ended up costing a lot more than the $150.

In the world of real estate and life, the world is small. You need friends and relationships, and those require grace and understanding. The measure of a relationship is not only found in the good times, but in the challenging times as well. Contractors, like you, aren't perfect. Agents, like you, aren't perfect. Lenders, like you, aren't perfect. Sellers and buyers, like you, aren't perfect. Use those imperfections as opportunities to build relationships with real people that will be on this real estate journey with you for a long time.

THE DEVIL IS IN THE DETAILS

I used to hate it when I renovated a home with my pops. It was always over budget and ran past schedule. We always had too many conversations and had to go over way too many details. Whenever we sat down to discuss the project, it was always about more money or another seemingly small detail we had to hash out. The result is that 100 percent of every home we bought or sold ended in success. There were no home inspection issues, homes sold fast and for top dollar, sales processes were smooth, and everyone was happy (agents, buyers, sellers, lenders).

The larger success was found in the small details. The seemingly small details made a big impact on the final outcome. The 15-minute strategy meetings over time made the four-month project a success. My pops had to change every light bulb, fix every issue, and make sure everything was perfect. He didn't do it because the buyer or seller might find out; he did it because it was his project, his home, and he had to live with the end product.

Often in real estate, when you want to control the big picture, the big outcome, we don't want to dive into the small details. At 100 percent of home inspections, we find small issues that turned into more costly problems over time. Servicing HVAC twice per year can save you money when you sell, but it can also save in energy costs. Adding gutter guards don't add value to your home, but they do keep gutters clean, which keeps water from running down into your basement. Changing the light bulbs in your rental won't increase your rent, but it will tell your tenant that you care about the small things and want to protect your investment.

I love when I'm working with a client, agent, or contractor that focuses on the small things. If they can handle the small issues of real estate, then I'm much more confident they can navigate the big issues. And those are the type of people I can do good business with.

BUILD YOUR TEAM BEFORE
YOU *NEED* YOUR TEAM

Success in real estate is found in the quality and depth of your relationships. We live in a world that's more interested in *what* than *who*. When I look around me, there have been key relationships that have helped me get to this level of real estate success.

- **Mentors:** Everyone is looking for someone that can help them make money in real estate. Many don't know how to build a quality relationship. New technology has made it easier to communicate, but many mistake that for building relationships. I've known all of my mentors in real estate for many years before I learned anything from them. I took the time to get to know them to determine if they would be the type of leader and teacher that could help me get better. I never paid for the relationship, but instead invested time and understanding in how I could help them and plant seeds in their life. Years later, I've seen, picked, and enjoyed the fruits of the harvest. Who can you plant seeds with today that will harvest good fruit in the future?

- **Contractors:** I love to find quality people that do quality work. Yes, I want a good deal, but I won't sacrifice a relationship over money. I asked people in the business who they like. I keep a part-time and full-time contractor on deck at all times; full time for my jobs that require a larger scope, and part time for those minor fixes that my big guy can't get to. I proactively refer business to my team, so that when my turn comes for service, they make sure I'm taken care of.

BONUS TIP:
Never have your contractors chase you for money. Pay them on time, and the relationship will always be rewarded.

- **Agents:** Same as with my contractors and mentors, having great relationships with agents is vital to being successful in any part of real estate. A great agent is a connector, a networker, a problem fixer and a lifeline when you need one. The best way to ensure you are taken care of is to take care of someone else. Agents don't just need referrals of your friends that are buying or selling, but opportunities for learning, quality contractor relationships, and simply LOVE. Yep, I said love. Call and check in on the person that is going to assist you in the largest financial transaction of your life.

- **Championships are won and enjoyed with a team.** Even if you are simply planning to own ONE home and live there for the rest of your life, you still need a team to help you keep your home in good condition. Additionally, if you are looking to make real estate investing a part of your retirement plan, building a quality team is important to your overall success.

FLIPPING VS. BUYING AND HOLDING

Turn on any TV network and you will see a flipping duo. The formula is the same: buying a distressed home below market value, renovating and fixing it up, and selling it for huge profits. But what are the two steps that the TV networks leave out? Can you guess?

It's the large capital gains tax that is now owed to Uncle Sam and that the investor now has to find another home and do it all over again. That cycle never ends.

Flipping is done for income; it's essentially a job.

Buying and holding is an investment that is built for long-term wealth. It's not sexy, and it's not normally on the TV networks, but it is the source of a majority of the wealth in the world of real estate.

I've always believed in passive cash flow over income. Cash flow works for you and compounds over time. The same energy and effort can be put to buying long-term investment properties as properties to flip, but why do most people want to flip? Because it's sexy and quick money, and everybody else is trying to do it. In the world of real estate, if it's sexy, quick money, and everybody is trying to do it, my rule of thumb is to stay away from it.

Let's look at a couple of different scenarios.

SCENARIO 1:
You have $100K to invest in real estate.
You flip two homes per year. (FYI: Flips are hard to find.)
You make $20K off each, so that's $40K per year.
You pay taxes at 35 percent, so you end up with $26K
(not a bad take).

SCENARIO 2:
Now, in the same market, you can buy and hold rentals.
With that $100K, you buy and hold four homes at $80K sales
price per home (adjust to your market).
With a down payment of $64K, you'll have money for
renovation (we will talk more about renovations for rentals later).
You finance 80 percent and put down 20 percent.
Properties give you cash flow of a modest $400 per month
($1,200 per month total).
That's $14,400 per year, *every year!* After five years, that's $72K.

Sure you could take that $26K from the previous scenario and reinvest it in other real estate opportunities over the course of the same five years and end up at $72K off your initial investment. But here's the catch: you'll have to work (ACTIVE) to grow that money every year from that point forward. With scenario #2, your initial investment will reap a return year over year with minimal to no work from you (PASSIVE).

Which would you choose?

Now these numbers are examples and may not work in your particular market, but I encourage you to at least explore and see if buying and holding for future wealth is worth your time and attention. I know what it has done for me and my family and what it can do for you. My goal is to get $50K in passive real estate income per month. I think I can live off of that! What's your goal? Start with that and work backwards.

This is important to me because retirement in the next 20 years will be much different than it was for our parents and grandparents. Pensions, Medicare/Medicaid, and retirement plans will not support your retirement; buying and holding real estate will. And if properly managed, it will be there for future generations.

THE FOUR WAYS TO MAKE MONEY IN REAL ESTATE INVESTING

There are four central ways to make money in real estate investing:

1. Monthly cash flow
2. Tax savings
3. Mortgage pay-down
4. Market appreciation

- **Monthly cash flow is the easiest to understand and quantify.** At its base, the formula looks something like this: *monthly rent - monthly mortgage - recurring expense = cash flow*. The question I am often asked on this subject is: How much should I expect in cash flow? My answer is that I don't know, and that question shouldn't be asked until you know your financial goals. Keep in mind those goals can change for you, depending on what season of life you're in. As a young investor, I was determined to get as much cash flow as possible, but now as I get older, wiser, and more financially seasoned, I focus more on tax shelter and mortgage pay-down.

- **Tax savings:** Now I don't profess to be a CPA or accounting genius, but real estate is a wonderful instrument for tax shelter. If you purchased and held properly, you should be able to find ways to reduce or differ how much you pay to good old Uncle Sam. Do yourself a favor: If you plan to buy real estate for wealth, hire a real-estate-centric accountant. If they are good, they will be worth every penny you pay them.

- **Mortgage pay-down:** This is often the most neglected area of real estate in my eyes. If you have *zero* market appreciation and make *zero* cash flow, you will still have a tenant paying down your mortgage and creating equity. I've been focusing on putting some of my properties into shorter-term mortgages and getting less cash flow now, so I can get more cash flow when I need it most (i.e., when I retire). Trust me, time flies, so making smart decisions now leads to better options later.

- **Market appreciation:** If you buy a good piece of real estate in a good area, it will likely appreciate without you doing much. On average, the housing real estate market goes up roughly 2 to 3 percent. Compounded over time, that is a significant amount of wealth. I could do the math for you, but I think it's important for you to do it. Grab a pen and do it! Take the average price of a home in your area and put 3 percent year over year on top of the cash flow, tax savings, and mortgage pay-down. It's a great formula for real estate investing success.

- **Trust me.** It's served my family well over the past 25 years, and it's the reason I'm sharing with you. #ThankMeLater

PAY IT FORWARD

WHY REAL ESTATE?

I'm often asked why I got into real estate. My story starts after graduating from George Mason University. I was looking for a job. I thought I wanted to sit behind a desk and do some technical writing/advertising, but after two weeks, I realized it wasn't for me. I ran across a buddy who recommended that I come by the car dealership and inquire about a sales position. By that weekend, I was selling my first of many cars, a red '94 Mazda Miata. I enjoyed my time and income at the car dealership and, after two years of success, was pushed by my financial advisor/mentor/father to buy a home. In full disclosure, I really wanted to continue renting. My good friend was my roommate, and we had a sweet bachelor pad in the Kingstowne area of Alexandria, Virginia. My dad pushed the issue and told me that he and my mother had been saving my college graduation present for me in the form of a $5K down payment. Of their many gifts to me, this was the most important gift I've received (Ok, maybe second most important since they also paid for 5 years of college tuition). This will be a tradition that we will continue for our own children.

He told me that they were coming up over the weekend and that I should get the newspaper to find open houses to visit. (Yes, young folks, that's the way we used to search for open houses: in the good old *Washington Post*.)

We visited several homes, and it became apparent that no one thought I was a serious buyer. Maybe it was the sweatpants, braids, or my youth, but no one would give us the time or attention. If they did, they'd talk to my parents and focus no energy on me. At the last home of the day, I met a sweet older lady who reminded me of my aunt. She agreed to take me to see some homes. I scheduled an appointment for my day off and showed up at the office, ready to buy. I sat in the lobby for 30 minutes while the receptionist tried to get her on the phone with no luck.

I left the office, went to the gym, and took this as a sign that I shouldn't buy a home.

I'll never forget that next day at the dealership. It was a Wednesday, normally a slow day at the dealership, and a young kid walked onto the lot. He looked younger than me, but I learned that you take everyone seriously because you never know. Within one hour, he found the car he wanted to buy, and we were getting the paperwork rolling. As he handed me his paperwork, I asked him what he did for a living. He smiled and said, "I'm a real estate agent." I looked up to the heavens, smiled, and mentioned, "God, you have a sense of humor." I let him know that he'd be helping me buy a home.

Six weeks later, I settled on my first home and had already completed my class to get my real estate license at Northern Virginia Community College.

With a newly purchased fixer-upper home and six months of saved income, I started my real estate career. My mission was to make sure that everyone who wanted to buy a home, and had the means to do so, had a respectful agent who they could go to and trust, someone who would respect them—exactly as they are.

It's been a blessed ride, and our firm still works every day to be a blessing to our clients, fellow agents, community, and friends.

ALLEN JOHNSON

BE A BLESSING FOUNDATION

The Be a Blessing Foundation is a faith-based organization dedicated to being a proactive blessing in the community. We partner with area professionals, business leaders, colleges, and community organizers to identify and provide solutions to community based issues. Our flagship program centers around youth mentorship and personal development. The foundation was founded by Allen Johnson, a lifelong community organizer and connector, to empower today's youth by giving them time, love, respect, and resources to live the life God wants for them. Our goal is to grow the community's students, stretch their minds, and show them that someone cares and expects them to excel in all areas of life. We believe an investment in these students will pay major dividends and will compound these values in our community and families. The topics covered in these sessions include: motivation, positivity, accountability, love, entrepreneurship, manners, respect, money management, being truthful, teamwork, self-control, goal setting, values, communication, conflict resolution, character development, self-esteem, social skills, and financial awareness.

The foundation works tirelessly to carry out this mission through empowerment outings, through emergency resource allocation, and by providing weekly mentoring to youth in the community. The foundation primarily works with fifth grade boys in Title 1 schools who have been identified by the school principal and/or school counselor as struggling socially and/or academically, but have the potential to be successful with the assistance of a strong mentor.

Are you willing to help be a blessing for others? Email us or visit www.BeABlessingDMV.org to find out how you can help!

ACKNOWLEDGMENTS

I grew up during in an era when it took a village to raise a king and my village has meant everything to my growth.

I want to thank my parents for never allowing me to think about anything less than excellence. I wake up everyday driven to build on your foundation.

Christal, my wife, life partner and soulmate. Thank you for making me a better man in every sense of the word.

My girls, Sydney and Camila, you have given me my purpose and passion. I now understand what the word love means.

Our clients over the past 18 years. You have allowed me to grow and supported this real estate mission. Thank you for believing in this country boy from central Virginia.

AJ Team family, past, present and future, thanks for allowing me to find my voice through teaching, leading, and learning from you.

George Mason University thanks for providing me a tribe and education that gave me the confidence to grow in so many ways.

Special thanks to Ashley Yarbrough for helping with the editing and creating my vision for this book.

Sarah Beaudin for your formatting, patience and guidance on this project.

To the rest of my village (way too many to mention) please know that I love you and thank you!